The Marathon, Not the Sprint

Building Lasting Wealth Through Patience

Andrew Galowey

Copyright © [Andrew Galowey] [2024]. All rights reserved. No part of this publication may be reproduced, distributed, or transmitted in any form or by any means, including photocopying, recording, or other electronic or mechanical methods, without the prior written permission of the publisher, except in the case of brief quotations embodied in critical reviews and certain other noncommercial uses permitted by copyright law.

Table Of Contents

Introduction

Chapter 1: Starting at the Beginning: Establishing Your Financial Foundation

Chapter 2: Slow and steady wins the race: cultivating patience for long-term growth

Chapter 3: The Power of Compound Interest: Put Your Wealth on Autopilot

Chapter 4: Building Your Investment Arsenal: Selecting Strategies for the Long Run

Chapter 5: Weathering the Storms: Maintaining Discipline During Market Fluctuations

Chapter 6: Crossing the Finish Line: Leading a Financially Secure Life

Introduction

Imagine yourself on the starting line of a marathon, not a sprint. The route to financial stability lies ahead of you, long and steady. This book is your guide, providing you with the information and mentality necessary to complete this marathon rather than a frenzied sprint.

"The Marathon, Not the Sprint" is not about flashy get-rich-quick schemes. It is about developing long-term wealth via patience, measured techniques, and the power of time. We'll look at ways to avoid impulsive choices, encourage long-term thinking, and use compound interest to consistently increase your money.

This path will not be without hurdles. The market may vary, presenting you with unexpected challenges. But with the correct tools and steadfast dedication, you'll be able to overcome these challenges and concentrate on your ultimate goal: a life of financial independence and security. So lace up your metaphorical running shoes and let's get started!

Chapter 1: Starting at the Beginning: Establishing Your Financial Foundation

The starting pistol goes off, and a flood of runners pushes ahead. Adrenaline rushes, muscles strain, and everyone wants to go ahead. But this is not a sprint; it is a marathon. A quick burst of speed may get you out of the starting blocks first, but it does not ensure success at the finish line. Building money is a comparable path that requires a long-term mindset and a focus on consistent, sustainable development.

This book is a guide to running the financial marathon, not the get-rich-quick sprint. We'll get away from the attraction of immediate success and look at ways for creating long-term wealth via patience, dedication, and wise preparation.

Before we lace up and hit the street, let's make sure we're prepared for the long haul. This chapter focuses on establishing a sound financial foundation, the base on which your wealth will be developed.

The Power of a Plan

Every successful marathon runner follows a training regimen. They recognize their own talents and shortcomings, create attainable objectives, and measure their progress. Creating riches takes a same technique. Your financial plan acts as a road map, detailing your objectives, tactics, and schedule for reaching them.

Begin by taking a critical look at your existing financial status. Monitor your income and spending for a month or two. Be honest: where is your money going? How much do you make and how much do you spend? This will assist you in identifying areas where you may reduce spending or save more money.

Next, set financial objectives. What do you hope your money will do for you in the short, medium, and long term? Are you saving for a dream trip, a down payment on a home, or a secure retirement? Setting specific objectives can help you stay focused and motivated as you navigate your financial path.

Building Your Emergency Fund

Assume you're halfway through the marathon, feeling great and making terrific progress. Suddenly, you twist your ankle. An unexpected medical expenditure might destroy your financial efforts just as easily. That is why maintaining a well-funded emergency savings account is critical.

This safety net should cover any unforeseen costs, such as auto repairs, medical bills, or job loss. Experts suggest saving 3-6 months' worth of living costs in your emergency fund. While this may be frightening at first, start small and progress gradually. Even a few hundred dollars is a good start, and with consistent contributions, you'll be astonished at how rapidly your emergency fund grows.

Conquering the Debt Monster

High-interest debt is a hefty burden to bear on your financial journey. Every dollar spent on interest payments reduces your ability to save for the future. Prioritize paying off high-interest debts such as credit cards and personal loans. Create a debt repayment plan and set aside a percentage of your monthly income to pay it down. There are several debt payback schemes, including the snowball and avalanche methods. Research and choose the one that best fits your financial circumstances and personality.

Mastering Your Money Habits.

Long-distance running demands discipline. You cannot eat every donut you see at a rest break and expect to finish strong. Building riches requires a comparable amount of self-control. Create good financial habits such as budgeting, comparing shopping, and avoiding impulsive purchases. Use free financial resources at your local library or online to learn how to manage your money wisely.

Investment for the Future

Finally, the most critical aspect of establishing a solid financial foundation is investing. Compound interest is the magic formula that converts little investments into substantial riches over time. Consider a snowball rolling down a hill; it begins tiny but gains velocity with each turn, increasing exponentially. That demonstrates the power of compound interest. Starting early, investing frequently, and allowing your money to grow over time can astound you at how much wealth you may build.

Chapter 1 is just the beginning. We've provided you with the fundamentals, including a financial plan, emergency reserves, a debt reduction strategy, and good spending habits. Now, let's look at the tools and tactics that can help you throughout your financial marathon trip.

Chapter 2: Slow and steady wins the race: cultivating patience for long-term growth

The clamor of the crowd diminishes as you relax into the marathon's cadence. The days of frenetic bursts of speed are over; today it's all about pacing yourself for the long haul. This principle underpins wealth creation. Patience is your most precious asset; pursuing rapid riches often ends in dangerous judgments and poor outcomes. This chapter explores the importance of patience and how it leads to long-term financial success.

The Allure of Get Rich Quick Schemes

Financial news bombards us with tales of instant billionaires and fresh investment ideas. It's tempting to imagine that there's a hidden shortcut to wealth, but the truth is considerably less glamorous. Get-rich-quick scams often entail substantial risk and a high likelihood of failure. Remember that if anything seems too good to be true, it generally is.

Investing is a marathon, not a casino risk. Focus on accumulating long-term wealth via steady, consistent growth. This takes discipline and the determination to sacrifice now enjoyment for a more secure future.

Taming the Emotional Roller Coaster

The financial markets are volatile. One day, your portfolio soars; the next, it plummets. These changes may be emotionally charged, prompting panic selling or rash investing choices.

This is when patience comes in. Resist the desire to respond to each market fluctuation. Remember, you're in it for the long haul. Short-term volatility is unavoidable, but long-term trends are generally good. Staying cool and focused on your long-term objectives can help you avoid making impulsive choices that might jeopardize your financial development.

Building a Diversified Portfolio

Imagine placing all of your eggs in one basket and then stumbling -- catastrophe! Similarly, depending on a single investment for future success is a dangerous strategy. Diversification is the foundation of a careful and wise investment plan.

Spread your assets among several asset types, such as equities, bonds, and real estate. This helps to reduce risk because if one asset class performs badly, another may remain stable or even flourish. Diversification also helps you to collect returns from a variety of market sectors, resulting in a more stable and resilient portfolio.

The Power of Compound Interest

Compound interest, according to Albert Einstein, is the "eighth wonder of the world." It is the alchemy that permits even tiny investments to increase dramatically over time. Here's a secret: your curiosity generates interest. Reinvesting your gains enables your money to snowball and expand enormously over time.

The sooner you begin investing, the longer your money has to profit from compound interest. Even tiny, persistent donations may build significant wealth over time. Patience enables you to use this enormous energy for long-term financial gain.

The time value of money

A dollar now is more valuable than a dollar tomorrow. The notion known as the time value of money emphasizes the significance of beginning early. Compound interest has a bigger effect on your money as it grows over time.

Assume you invest $1,000 yearly with a 7% annual return. Over 20 years, it equates to around $58,433. Now, if you wait ten years before investing, you'll end up with a substantially lesser sum. Patience helps you to capitalize on the time worth of money and enhance your long-term earnings.

Building Wealth is a Marathon, not a Sprint.

Developing patience is key for navigating the financial markets and attaining long-term financial success. Resist the need for quick satisfaction and instead concentrate on increasing wealth via gradual, consistent development. By diversifying your portfolio, beginning early, and remaining disciplined throughout market changes, you may use compound interest and time to reach your long-term financial objectives. Remember that patience pays off, particularly when it comes to accumulating money.

Chapter 3: The Power of Compound Interest: Put Your Wealth on Autopilot

Consider this: you plant a little seed in the earth. With patience, sunshine, and water, the seed grows into a majestic tree, towering above you with power and beauty. Compound interest operates in a similar manner. It's the secret sauce that transforms little investments into substantial riches over time, silently operating in the background, almost on autopilot. This chapter digs into the power of compound interest and how to use it to your financial advantage.

The snowball effect

Have you ever seen a snowball tumble down a snowy hill? It begins little, but with each rotation, it collects more snow, expanding rapidly in size. Compound interest acts similarly. When you invest your money, it begins collecting interest. This money is then reinvested, generating interest on itself. This causes a snowball effect, in which your money accumulates at a rapid pace over time.

Let's start with a basic example. Assume you invest $1,000 with a 5% yearly interest rate. In the first year, you'll make $50 in interest. Now the magic occurs. In the second year, you get interest on both the initial $1,000 and the $50 you earned the year before. This snowball effect continues year after year, dramatically increasing your total returns.

The Value of Starting Early

The sooner you begin investing, the longer your money has to profit from compound interest. Even tiny, persistent donations may build significant wealth over time. Consider two people, Sarah and Ben, who each start with $1,000 and invest yearly at a 7% return. Sarah starts at 25 and invests for 40 years, while Ben begins at 35 and invests for 30 years.

Sarah will have an astounding $324,338 at retirement, while Ben will have a reasonable $132,673. What's the difference? Sarah spent ten years for compound interest to work its magic. This basic example demonstrates the value of beginning early. Compound interest has a bigger effect on your money as it grows over time.

The Beauty of Consistent Contributions

You don't need a large money to gain from compound interest. Consistency is essential. Making little contributions on a regular basis might have a startling long-term effect. Even if you simply have a few hundred dollars to invest each month, compound interest will work wonders.

Consider it like watering your seed every day. These tiny, persistent activities result in enormous development over time. As your income rises, you may progressively raise your contributions, hastening your wealth building.

The Mathematics Behind the Magic

Understanding the fundamental formula for compound interest might help you appreciate its power. Here is the formula:

$A = P(1 + r)^t$

Where:

A represents the future worth of your investment (the amount you'll have in the end).
P represents the first primary amount you deposit (your seed money).
r represents the yearly interest rate (growth rate).
t represents the number of years your investment increases.

By entering various variables, you may observe how variations in interest rates and investment duration affect your ultimate sum. This may be an effective tool for establishing realistic objectives and assessing the potential of your assets.

Using the Power of Automation

Technology may help you generate money via compound interest. Consider setting up automatic transfers between your checking and investing accounts. This assures constant donations while eliminating the temptation to spend the money elsewhere. By automating your investments, you enable compound interest to operate effortlessly in the background.

Compound Interest: The Path to Financial Freedom

Compound interest is a great instrument for achieving long-term financial independence.

Starting early, investing regularly, and using the power of automation may help you build your wealth immensely. Remember that compound interest is your quiet companion, working persistently behind the scenes to provide your financial security. Let it be your secret weapon in the marathon of creating long-term wealth.

Chapter 4: Building Your Investment Arsenal: Selecting Strategies for the Long Run

You've worked hard, improved your endurance, and accepted patience. Now it's time to choose the appropriate shoes for the terrain ahead. In the marathon of wealth accumulation, your "shoes" are your investing strategy. This chapter looks at numerous investing possibilities to help you choose the ones that are most suited to your long-term objectives and risk tolerance.

Understanding Your Risk Tolerance

Think about a rollercoaster ride. Some individuals like the adrenaline rush of steep drops and abrupt twists, while others prefer a more leisurely, picturesque tour. Similarly, investors have various risk tolerances. Understanding your own risk tolerance is critical when selecting investment vehicles.

Risk and reward are interrelated. In general, greater-return investments involve a higher level of risk. In contrast, investments with lesser prospective returns are often seen to be safer.

Evaluate your risk tolerance. Are you an experienced investor who can handle market volatility, or are you risk-averse and emphasize money preservation? This self-assessment will help you choose appropriate investing alternatives.

Investment All-Stars: A Look at Popular Options

The financial environment provides a varied variety of alternatives. Let's look at some common choices:

- Stocks: Purchasing shares of a firm offers you a stake in its ownership and future earnings. Stocks have the potential to provide huge profits, but they also involve the danger of substantial losses.

- Bonds: Bonds are essentially loans made to governments or enterprises that provide regular interest payments and repayment of the principle amount at maturity. They are typically regarded less risky than stocks, although they have lesser potential rewards.

Mutual funds and ETFs are professionally managed portfolios of stocks, bonds, and other assets. They provide diversification and ease, letting you to invest in many assets with a single transaction. Mutual funds and ETFs are also viable options for individuals looking for a more controlled investment strategy.

Investing in real estate may be a profitable way to accumulate money. Owning rental properties offers a consistent source of income as well as the opportunity for value appreciation. However, real estate requires large initial investment and continuing maintenance obligations.

Matching Your Investments with Your Goals

Different investment instruments serve different purposes. Are you saving for a short-term objective, like a vehicle down payment, or a long-term one, such as retirement?

Consider short-term choices such as high-yield savings accounts or certificates of deposit (CDs), which provide reduced risks and assured returns.

For long-term objectives, equities and stock-based mutual funds or ETFs have the potential for more gain, but at a higher risk.

Remember that a well-diversified portfolio that balances risk and reward is critical to long-term success.

Asset Allocation: Spread Your Bets

Just as you wouldn't put all of your eggs in one basket, you shouldn't invest only in one asset class. Diversification is the gold standard of investment. You may reduce risk by diversifying your assets among asset types such as stocks, bonds, and real estate.

There is no one-size-fits-all solution to asset allocation. Your appropriate blend will be determined by your risk tolerance, age, and financial objectives. A younger investor with a high risk tolerance may allocate more of their portfolio to equities, while someone approaching retirement may prefer bonds for income and stability.

Rebalance Your Portfolio

Market circumstances may cause the weightings of your assets to vary over time. For example, if the stock market does very well, your portfolio allocation may become more strongly weighted toward equities than was anticipated.

Rebalancing entails selling outperforming assets and buying more underperforming ones. This helps you maintain your chosen asset allocation while also managing risk during your financial journey.

Selecting the Right Investment Professionals

When navigating the investing environment, consider getting advice from financial experts or robo-advisors. Financial advisers provide specialized financial advice based on your unique requirements and objectives. Robo-advisors are automated investing platforms that provide low-cost, algorithm-driven portfolio management.

Investing for the long haul

Creating money is a marathon, not a sprint. Understanding your risk tolerance, aligning your assets to your objectives, and keeping a diverse portfolio are all necessary for selecting the best investing methods. Making educated judgments and keeping disciplined along your path can help you achieve your long-term financial goals. Remember, the investing possibilities offered here are just a starting point. Further study and expert advice may assist you in developing a personalized investment strategy that will move you ahead on your journey to financial independence.

Chapter 5: Weathering the Storms: Maintaining Discipline During Market Fluctuations

The crowd's enthusiasm diminish as you hit a part of the marathon known for high winds and unpredictable weather. Just as a runner must adjust to shifting circumstances, you will undoubtedly encounter times of market turbulence on your wealth-building trip. This chapter provides you with tactics for navigating these storms and remaining disciplined in the face of market changes.

Understanding Market Volatility

The financial markets do not follow a steady, predictable course. Periods of rapid expansion may be followed by abrupt downturns. This intrinsic volatility might be unsettling, but it is an expected component of the investing cycle. Don't misinterpret short-term variations as a permanent decrease.

Economic news, geopolitical events, and investor attitude are all potential sources of market volatility. While you cannot control external factors, you can influence how you respond to them.

The Emotional Roller Coaster

Watching your portfolio's value collapse may be emotionally upsetting. Fear and fear may impair your judgment, resulting in rash judgments that threaten your long-term financial objectives. Here's how to be cool and collected during market turbulence:

- Focus on Your Long-Term Goals: Remember that you are investing for a secure future, not for quick rewards. Keep your long-term objectives in mind and avoid making judgments based on short-term market volatility.

- Separate Emotions from financial Decisions: Don't allow fear or greed

30

drive your financial decisions. Create a clear investing plan based on your risk tolerance and adhere to it, even when emotions are strong.

- Limit News Consumption: Constant exposure to poor financial news might exacerbate anxiety. Instead, concentrate on keeping educated without being overwhelmed.

Maintaining Discipline During Downturns

Market downturns may challenge your discipline. Here are some techniques for remaining focused during turbulent periods:

- Do not panic sell: Selling your assets during a slump locks in your losses. Remember that the market has typically recovered after each slump. Stay invested and let your wealth recover over time.

- Maintain Consistent Contributions: Do not allow market swings disturb your investing strategy. Continue making regular payments, which may even enable you to buy additional shares at a lower price during a downturn (dollar-cost averaging).

- Rebalance if Necessary: If market swings substantially affect your asset allocation, you should consider rebalancing your portfolio to preserve your intended risk profile.

Remember your risk tolerance.

Your risk tolerance is critical in dealing with market volatility. If you are willing to take on a high level of risk, you may be able to withstand substantial losses. Someone with a lower risk tolerance, on the other hand, may choose to temporarily modify their asset allocation in order to limit exposure to turbulent markets.

Looking behind the headlines:

Financial news often focuses on short-term market fluctuations. Instead, concentrate on the long-term fundamentals of the economy and the firms you've invested in. Strong firms with sound financials are more likely to survive market disasters and emerge stronger in the long run.

Diversification: Your Protection Against Volatility

Remember the golden rule of investing: diversify. By diversifying your assets across asset classes, you reduce the effect of a single downturn. Even if one asset class performs badly, others may remain stable or even flourish, reducing the total effect on your portfolio.

Knowledge is power.

The more you know about markets and how they work, the more prepared you will be to withstand volatility. Make time to study about various asset classes, investing methods, and historical market cycles. Knowledge may help you make educated judgments and prevent knee-jerk responses during challenging times.

Market volatility is a marathon—not a sprint.

Just as a marathon runner must prepare for adverse weather conditions, so should you prepare for market volatility on your path to success. By cultivating a long-term mindset, regulating your emotions, and being disciplined throughout downturns, you'll be well-positioned to weather the storms and emerge triumphant in the financial marathon. Remember that market volatility are just transient, while your long-term investing objectives stay consistent. Stay focused and cool, and let your well-built portfolio withstand the storm.

Chapter 6: Crossing the Finish Line: Leading a Financially Secure Life

As you approach the last bend, the crowd's clamor becomes more intense. Months of training, numerous kilometers ran, and unshakable commitment have culminated in this moment. Crossing the finish line of a marathon represents a triumph of endurance and planning. Building riches has a comparable victory. This chapter delves into the benefits of your patience, discipline, and the delicious taste of financial independence.

Financial freedom is more than just money

Financial security is more than simply having a big bank account. It's about having peace of mind, knowing you have the means to meet your necessities and pursue your aspirations. It is the ability to choose how you spend your time, whether working a rewarding part-time job or following a passion project. It's the capacity to withstand unforeseen financial setbacks without worry of losing your house or security.

The Benefits of Long-Term Planning

Reaching your financial objectives, whether they be early retirement, a comfortable living cost cushion, or supporting your child's college, is quite satisfying. Years of continuous budgeting, sensible investments, and delayed pleasure result in a feeling of security and freedom that you would not have otherwise had.

Security for You and Your Loved Ones

Financial stability helps you to look for yourself and your loved ones. Having a sound financial foundation brings peace of mind. You may prepare for your future healthcare requirements, assist your children with their schooling, and support elderly parents without incurring financial hardship.

Freedom to explore

Financial stability offers up new opportunities. Maybe it's finally taking that dream trip, creating your own company, or doing volunteer work you care about. Without financial constraints, you may follow your passions and explore life's potential.

The Power of Giving Back

Financial stability enables you to be a donor. Donate to a cause that is important to you, or help a local charity. Witnessing the effect of your charity provides a feeling of satisfaction that extends beyond worldly goods.

Living a Life with Less Stress

Financial issues are a major cause of stress. Knowing you have a stable financial future alleviates that strain. You may enjoy life's pleasures without always worrying about bills and unforeseen costs.

Remember: the journey is just as important.

Building long-term wealth is a marathon, not a sprint. While crossing the finish line is a reason for joy, the trip itself is very valuable. Lessons learnt, discipline gained, and a feeling of success all contribute to a more meaningful existence.

Financial Security is a continuous journey.

You can't stop preparing just because you've reached your financial objectives. Your financial strategy may need to be adjusted when life circumstances change. Regularly examine your objectives, rebalance your portfolio as appropriate, and adjust your strategy to changing conditions.

Maintaining financial discipline.

Maintaining financial stability, like keeping healthy, involves continual work and discipline. Avoid lifestyle inflation, which occurs when you spend more as your income increases. Even after you've met your financial objectives, continue to make wise choices and emphasize saving and investing.

Share Your Knowledge.

Financial knowledge enables others. Spread your financial expertise among your family and friends. Help them build good money habits and support them on their own paths to financial stability.

The finish line is only the beginning.

Financial stability is not the finish, but rather a new beginning. It is a platform from which you may follow your interests, live life to the fullest, and make a good difference in the world.

You've completed the process of accumulating long-term wealth. Celebrate your accomplishments, but keep in mind that the path to financial stability is never-ending. Keep learning, improving, and making sound financial choices. With steadfast dedication and a long-term mindset, you've ensured a future full of freedom, stability, and limitless possibilities.

www.ingramcontent.com/pod-product-compliance
Lightning Source LLC
Chambersburg PA
CBHW050249230526
45470CB00005B/2176